MEADOWLANDS

ALSO BY LOUISE GLÜCK

MEADOWLANDS

LOUISE GLÜCK

THE ECCO PRESS

THE ECCO PRESS
100 West Broad Street
Hopewell, New Jersey 08525

Published simultaneously in Canada
by Penguin Books Canada Ltd., Ontario
Printed in the United States of America

Many thanks to the following publications in which some of these poems first
appeared: *Antaeus*, *The New Yorker*, *Ploughshares*, *The Threepenny Review*, and *Agni Review*.

Library of Congress Cataloging-in-Publication Data

Glück, Louise, 1943–
     Meadowlands / Louise Glück.—1st ed.
       p.   cm.
     ISBN 0-88001-452-0
     ISBN 0-88001-506-3 (paperback)
     I. Title.
   PS3557.L8M4   1996
   811'.54—dc 20   95-33526

Designed by Fearn Cutler de Vicq de Cumptich

The text of this book is set in Bembo

9 8 7 6 5 4 3 2

FIRST EDITION

TO ROBERT AND FRANK

CONTENTS

Let's play choosing music. Favorite form.

Opera.

Favorite work.

Figaro. No. Figaro and Tannhauser. Now
it's your turn: sing one for me.

MEADOWLANDS

PENELOPE'S SONG

Little soul, little perpetually undressed one,
do now as I bid you, climb
the shelf-like branches of the spruce tree;
wait at the top, attentive, like
a sentry or look-out. He will be home soon;
it behooves you to be
generous. You have not been completely
perfect either; with your troublesome body
you have done things you shouldn't
discuss in poems. Therefore
call out to him over the open water, over the bright water
with your dark song, with your grasping,
unnatural song—passionate,
like Maria Callas. Who
wouldn't want you? Whose most demonic appetite
could you possibly fail to answer? Soon
he will return from wherever he goes in the meantime,
suntanned from his time away, wanting
his grilled chicken. Ah, you must greet him,
you must shake the boughs of the tree
to get his attention,
but carefully, carefully, lest
his beautiful face be marred
by too many falling needles.

CANA

What can I tell you that you don't know
that will make you tremble again?

Forsythia
by the roadside, by
wet rocks, on the embankments
underplanted with hyacinth—

For ten years I was happy.
You were there; in a sense,
you were always with me, the house, the garden
constantly lit,
not with light as we have in the sky
but with those emblems of light
which are more powerful, being
implicitly some earthly
thing transformed—

And all of it vanished,
reabsorbed into impassive process. Then
what will we see by,
now that the yellow torches have become
green branches?

QUIET EVENING

You take my hand; then we're alone
in the life-threatening forest. Almost immediately

we're in a house; Noah's
grown and moved away; the clematis after ten years
suddenly flowers white.

More than anything in the world
I love these evenings when we're together,
the quiet evenings in summer, the sky still light at this hour.

So Penelope took the hand of Odysseus,
not to hold him back but to impress
this peace on his memory:

from this point on, the silence through which you move
is my voice pursuing you.

CEREMONY

I stopped liking artichokes when I stopped eating
butter. Fennel
I never liked.

One thing I've always hated
about you: I hate that you refuse
to have people at the house. Flaubert
had more friends and Flaubert
was a recluse.

> Flaubert was crazy: he lived
> with his mother.

Living with you is like living
at boarding school:
chicken Monday, fish Tuesday.

> I have deep friendships.
> I have friendships
> with other recluses.

> Why do you call it rigidity?
> Can't you call it a taste
> for ceremony? Or is your hunger for beauty
> completely satisfied by your own person?

Another thing: name one other person
who doesn't have furniture.

We have fish Tuesday
because it's fresh Tuesday. If I could drive
we could have it different days.

If you're so desperate
for precedent, try
Stevens. Stevens
never traveled; that doesn't mean
he didn't know pleasure.

Pleasure maybe but not
joy. When you make artichokes,
make them for yourself.

PARABLE OF THE KING

The great king looking ahead
saw not fate but simply
dawn glittering over
the unknown island: as a king
he thought in the imperative—best
not to reconsider direction, best
to keep going forward
over the radiant water. Anyway,
what is fate but a strategy for ignoring
history, with its moral
dilemmas, a way of regarding
the present, where decisions
are made, as the necessary
link between the past (images of the king
as a young prince) and the glorious future (images
of slave girls). Whatever
it was ahead, why did it have to be
so blinding? Who could have known
that wasn't the usual sun
but flames rising over a world
about to become extinct?

MOONLESS NIGHT

A lady weeps at a dark window.
Must we say what it is? Can't we simply say
a personal matter? It's early summer;
next door the Lights are practising klezmer music.
A good night: the clarinet is in tune.

As for the lady—she's going to wait forever;
there's no point in watching longer.
After awhile, the streetlight goes out.

But is waiting forever
always the answer? Nothing
is always the answer; the answer
depends on the story.

Such a mistake to want
clarity above all things. What's
a single night, especially
one like this, now so close to ending?
On the other side, there could be anything,
all the joy in the world, the stars fading,
the streetlight becoming a bus stop.

DEPARTURE

The night isn't dark; the world is dark.
Stay with me a little longer.

Your hands on the back of the chair—
that's what I'll remember.
Before that, lightly stroking my shoulders.
Like a man training himself to avoid the heart.

In the other room, the maid discreetly
putting out the light I read by.

That room with its chalk walls—
how will it look to you I wonder
once your exile begins? I think your eyes will seek out
its light as opposed to the moon.
Apparently, after so many years, you need
distance to make plain its intensity.

Your hands on the chair, stroking
my body and the wood in exactly the same way.
Like a man who wants to feel longing again,
who prizes longing above all other emotion.

On the beach, voices of the Greek farmers,
impatient for sunrise.
As though dawn will change them
from farmers into heroes.

And before that, you are holding me because you are going away—
these are statements you are making,

not questions needing answers.

How can I know you love me
unless I see you grieve over me?

ITHACA

The beloved doesn't
need to live. The beloved
lives in the head. The loom
is for the suitors, strung up
like a harp with white shroud-thread.

He was two people.
He was the body and voice, the easy
magnetism of a living man, and then
the unfolding dream or image
shaped by the woman working the loom,
sitting there in a hall filled
with literal-minded men.

As you pity
the deceived sea that tried
to take him away forever
and took only the first,
the actual husband, you must
pity these men: they don't know
what they're looking at;
they don't know that when one loves this way
the shroud becomes a wedding dress.

TELEMACHUS' DETACHMENT

When I was a child looking
at my parents' lives, you know
what I thought? I thought
heartbreaking. Now I think
heartbreaking, but also
insane. Also
very funny.

PARABLE OF THE HOSTAGES

The Greeks are sitting on the beach
wondering what to do when the war ends. No one
wants to go home, back
to that bony island; everyone wants a little more
of what there is in Troy, more
life on the edge, that sense of every day as being
packed with surprises. But how to explain this
to the ones at home to whom
fighting a war is a plausible
excuse for absence, whereas
exploring one's capacity for diversion
is not. Well, this can be faced
later; these
are men of action, ready to leave
insight to the women and children.
Thinking things over in the hot sun, pleased
by a new strength in their forearms, which seem
more golden than they did at home, some
begin to miss their families a little,
to miss their wives, to want to see
if the war has aged them. And a few grow
slightly uneasy: what if war
is just a male version of dressing up,
a game devised to avoid
profound spiritual questions? Ah,
but it wasn't only the war. The world had begun
calling them, an opera beginning with the war's
loud chords and ending with the floating aria of the sirens.
There on the beach, discussing the various
timetables for getting home, no one believed
it could take ten years to get back to Ithaca;

no one foresaw that decade of insoluble dilemmas—oh unanswerable
affliction of the human heart: how to divide
the world's beauty into acceptable
and unacceptable loves! On the shores of Troy,
how could the Greeks know
they were hostage already: who once
delays the journey is
already enthralled; how could they know
that of their small number
some would be held forever by the dreams of pleasure,
some by sleep, some by music?

RAINY MORNING

You don't love the world.
If you loved the world you'd have
images in your poems.

John loves the world. He has
a motto: judge not
lest ye be judged. Don't

argue this point
on the theory it isn't possible
to love what one refuses
to know: to refuse

speech is not
to suppress perception.

Look at John, out in the world,
running even on a miserable day
like today. Your
staying dry is like the cat's pathetic
preference for hunting dead birds: completely

consistent with your tame spiritual themes,
autumn, loss, darkness, etc.

We can all write about suffering
with our eyes closed. You should show people
more of yourself; show them your clandestine
passion for red meat.

PARABLE OF THE TRELLIS

A clematis grew at the foot of a great trellis.
Despite being
modeled on a tree, the trellis
was a human invention; every year, in May,
the green wires of the struggling vine
climbed the straightforward
trellis, and after many years
white flowers burst from the brittle wood, like
a star shower from the heart of the garden.

Enough of that ruse. We both know
how the vine grows without
the trellis, how it sneaks
along the ground; we have both seen it
flower there, the white blossoms
like headlights growing out of a snake.

This isn't what the vine wants.
Remember, to the vine, the trellis
was never an image of confinement:
this is not
diminishment or tragedy.

The vine has a dream of light:
what is life in the dirt
with its dark freedoms
compared to supported ascent?

And for a time,
every summer we could see the vine
relive this decision, thus

obscuring the wood, structure
beautiful in itself, like
a harbor or willow tree.

TELEMACHUS' GUILT

Patience of the sort my mother
practised on my father
(which in his self-
absorption he mistook
for tribute though it was in fact
a species of rage—didn't he
ever wonder why he was
so blocked in expressing
his native abandon?): it infected
my childhood. Patiently
she fed me; patiently
she supervised the kindly
slaves who attended me, regardless
of my behavior, an assumption
I tested with increasing
violence. It seemed clear to me
that from her perspective
I didn't exist, since
my actions had
no power to disturb her: I was
the envy of my playmates.
In the decades that followed
I was proud of my father
for staying away
even if he stayed away for
the wrong reasons;
I used to smile
when my mother wept.
I hope now she could
forgive that cruelty; I hope
she understood how like

her own coldness it was,
a means of remaining
separate from what
one loves deeply.

ANNIVERSARY

I said you could snuggle. That doesn't mean
your cold feet all over my dick.

Someone should teach you how to act in bed.
What I think is you should
keep your extremities to yourself.

Look what you did—
you made the cat move.

       But I didn't want your hand there.
       I wanted your hand here.

       You should pay attention to my feet.
       You should picture them
       the next time you see a hot fifteen year old.
       Because there's a lot more where those feet come from.

I wish we went on walks
like Steven and Kathy; then
we'd be happy. You can even see it
in the dog.

     We don't have a dog.
     We have a hostile cat.

     I think Sam's
     intelligent; he
     resents being a pet.

     Why is it always family with you?
     Can't we ever be two adults?

Look how happy Captain is, how
at peace in the world. Don't you love
how he sits on the lawn, staring up at the birds? He thinks
because he's white they can't see him.

You know why they're happy? They take
the children. And you know why they can go
on walks with children? Because
they *have* children.

     They're nothing like us; they don't
     travel. That's why they have a dog.

Have you noticed how Alissa always comes back from the walks
holding something, bringing nature

into the house? Flowers in spring,
sticks in winter.

        I bet they're still taking the dog
        when the children are grown up.
        He's a young dog, practically
        a puppy.

        If we don't expect
        Sam to follow, couldn't we
        take him along?
        You could hold him.

TELEMACHUS' KINDNESS

When I was younger I felt
sorry for myself
compulsively; in practical terms,
I had no father; my mother
lived at her loom hypothesizing
her husband's erotic life; gradually
I realized no child on that island had
a different story; my trials
were the general rule, common
to all of us, a bond
among us, therefore
with humanity: what
a life my mother had, without
compassion for my father's
suffering, for a soul
ardent by nature, thus
ravaged by choice, nor had my father
any sense of her courage, subtly
expressed as inaction, being
himself prone to dramatizing,
to acting out: I found
I could share these perceptions
with my closest friends, as they shared
theirs with me, to test them,
to refine them: as a grown man
I can look at my parents
impartially and pity them both: I hope
always to be able to pity them.

PARABLE OF THE BEAST

The cat circles the kitchen
with the dead bird,
its new possession.

Someone should discuss
ethics with the cat as it
inquires into the limp bird:

in this house
we do not experience
will in this manner.

Tell that to the animal,
its teeth already
deep in the flesh of another animal.

MIDNIGHT

Speak to me, aching heart: what
ridiculous errand are you inventing for yourself
weeping in the dark garage
with your sack of garbage: it is not your job
to take out the garbage, it is your job
to empty the dishwasher. You are showing off again,
exactly as you did in childhood—where
is your sporting side, your famous
ironic detachment? A little moonlight hits
the broken window, a little summer moonlight, tender
murmurs from the earth with its ready sweetnesses—
is this the way you communicate
with your husband, not answering
when he calls, or is this the way the heart
behaves when it grieves: it wants to be
alone with the garbage? If I were you,
I'd think ahead. After fifteen years,
his voice could be getting tired; some night
if you don't answer, someone else will answer.

SIREN

I became a criminal when I fell in love.
Before that I was a waitress.

I didn't want to go to Chicago with you.
I wanted to marry you, I wanted
your wife to suffer.

I wanted her life to be like a play
in which all the parts are sad parts.

Does a good person
think this way? I deserve

credit for my courage—

I sat in the dark on your front porch.
Everything was clear to me:
if your wife wouldn't let you go
that proved she didn't love you.
If she loved you
wouldn't she want you happy?

I think now
if I felt less I would be
a better person. I was
a good waitress,
I could carry eight drinks.

I used to tell you my dreams.
Last night I saw a woman sitting in a dark bus—
in the dream, she's weeping, the bus she's on

is moving away. With one hand
she's waving; the other strokes
an egg carton full of babies.

The dream doesn't rescue the maiden.

Alissa isn't bringing back
sticks for the house; the sticks
belong to the dog.

MARINA

My heart was a stone wall
you broke through anyway.

My heart was an island garden
about to be trampled by you.

You didn't want my heart;
you were on your way to my body.

None of it was my fault.
You were everything to me,
not just beauty and money.
When we made love
the cat went to another bedroom.

Then you forgot me.

Not for no reason
did the stones
tremble around the walled garden:

there's nothing there now
except the wildness people call nature,
the chaos that takes over.

You took me to a place
where I could see the evil in my character
and left me there.

The abandoned cat
wails in the empty bedchamber.

PARABLE OF THE DOVE

A dove lived in a village.
When it opened its mouth
sweetness came out, sound
like a silver light around
the cherry bough. But
the dove wasn't satisfied.

It saw the villagers
gathered to listen under
the blossoming tree.
It didn't think: I
am higher than they are.
It wanted to walk among them,
to experience the violence of human feeling,
in part for its song's sake.

So it became human.
It found passion, it found violence,
first conflated, then
as separate emotions
and these were not
contained by music. Thus
its song changed,
the sweet notes of its longing to be human
soured and flattened. Then

the world drew back; the mutant
fell from love
as from the cherry branch,

it fell stained with the bloody
fruit of the tree.

So it is true after all, not merely
a rule of art:
change your form and you change your nature.
And time does this to us.

TELEMACHUS' DILEMMA

I can never decide
what to write on
my parents' tomb. I know
what he wants: he wants
beloved, which is
certainly to the point, particularly
if we count all
the women. But
that leaves my mother
out in the cold. She tells me
this doesn't matter to her
in the least; she prefers
to be represented by
her own achievement. It seems
tactless to remind them
that one does not
honor the dead by perpetuating
their vanities, their
projections of themselves.
My own taste dictates
accuracy without
garrulousness; they are
my parents, consequently
I see them together,
sometimes inclining to
husband and wife, other times
to *opposing forces.*

How could the Giants name
that place the Meadowlands? It has
about as much in common with a pasture
as would the inside of an oven.

New Jersey
was rural. They want you
to remember that.

Simms
was not a thug. LT
was not a thug.

What I think is we should
look at our surroundings
realistically, for what they are
in the present.

That's what
I tell you about the house.

No giant
would talk the way you talk.
You'd be a nicer person
if you were a fan of something.
When you do that with your mouth
you look like your mother.

You know what they are?
Kings among men.

So what king
fired Simms?

THE ROCK

Insignia
of the earth's
terrible recesses, spirit
of darkness, of
the criminal mind, I feel
certain there is within you
something human, to be
approached in speech. How else
did you approach Eve
with your addictive
information? I have paid
bitterly for her
lapse, therefore
attend to me. Tell me
how you live in hell,
what is required in hell,
for I would send
my beloved there. Not
of course forever:
I may want him
back sometime, not
permanently harmed but
severely chastened,
as he has not been, here
on the surface. What
shall I give him for
protection, what
shield that will not
wholly screen him? You must be
his guide and master: help him
shed his skin

as you do, though in this case
we want him
older underneath, maybe
a little mousy. I feel confident
you understand these
subtleties—you seem
so interested, you do not
slide back under your rock! Oh
I am sure we are somehow related
even if you are not
human; perhaps I have
the soul of a reptile after all.

CIRCE'S POWER

I never turned anyone into a pig.
Some people are pigs; I make them
look like pigs.

I'm sick of your world
that lets the outside disguise the inside.

Your men weren't bad men;
undisciplined life
did that to them. As pigs,

under the care of
me and my ladies, they
sweetened right up.

Then I reversed the spell,
showing you my goodness
as well as my power. I saw

we could be happy here,
as men and women are
when their needs are simple. In the same breath,

I foresaw your departure,
your men with my help braving
the crying and pounding sea. You think

a few tears upset me? My friend,
every sorceress is
a pragmatist at heart; nobody

sees essence who can't
face limitation. If I wanted only to hold you

I could hold you prisoner.

TELEMACHUS' FANTASY

Sometimes I wonder about my father's
years on those islands: why
was he so attractive
to women? He was in straits then, I suppose
desperate. I believe
women like to see a man
still whole, still standing, but
about to go to pieces: such
disintegration reminds them
of passion. I think of them as living
their whole lives
completely undressed. It must have
dazzled him, I think, women
so much younger than he was
evidently wild for him, ready
to do anything he wished. Is it
fortunate to encounter circumstances
so responsive to one's own will, to live
so many years
unquestioned, unthwarted? One
would have to believe oneself
entirely good or worthy. I
suppose in time either
one becomes a monster or
the beloved sees what one is. I never
wish for my father's life
nor have I any idea
what he sacrificed
to survive that moment. Less dangerous
to believe he was drawn to them
and so stayed

to see who they were. I think, though,
as an imaginative man
to some extent he
became who they were.

PARABLE OF FLIGHT

A flock of birds leaving the side of the mountain.
Black against the spring evening, bronze in early summer,
rising over blank lake water.

Why is the young man disturbed suddenly,
his attention slipping from his companion?
His heart is no longer wholly divided; he's trying to think
how to say this compassionately.

Now we hear the voices of the others, moving through the library
toward the veranda, the summer porch; we see them
taking their usual places on the various hammocks and chairs,
the white wood chairs of the old house, rearranging
the striped cushions.

Does it matter where the birds go? Does it even matter
what species they are?
They leave here, that's the point,
first their bodies, then their sad cries.
And from that moment, cease to exist for us.

You must learn to think of our passion that way.
Each kiss was real, then
each kiss left the face of the earth.

ODYSSEUS' DECISION

The great man turns his back on the island.
Now he will not die in paradise
nor hear again
the lutes of paradise among the olive trees,
by the clear pools under the cypresses. Time

begins now, in which he hears again
that pulse which is the narrative
sea, at dawn when its pull is strongest.
What has brought us here
will lead us away; our ship
sways in the tinted harbor water.

Now the spell is ended.
Give him back his life,
sea that can only move forward.

There was an apple tree in the yard—
this would have been
forty years ago—behind,
only meadow. Drifts
of crocus in the damp grass.
I stood at that window:
late April. Spring
flowers in the neighbor's yard.
How many times, really, did the tree
flower on my birthday,
the exact day, not
before, not after? Substitution
of the immutable
for the shifting, the evolving.
Substitution of the image
for relentless earth. What
do I know of this place,
the role of the tree for decades
taken by a bonsai, voices
rising from the tennis courts—
Fields. Smell of the tall grass, new cut.
As one expects of a lyric poet.
We look at the world once, in childhood.
The rest is memory.

THE BUTTERFLY

Look, a butterfly. Did you make a wish?

    You don't wish on butterflies.

You do so. Did you make one?

    Yes.

It doesn't count.

CIRCE'S TORMENT

I regret bitterly
the years of loving you in both
your presence and absence, regret
the law, the vocation
that forbid me to keep you, the sea
a sheet of glass, the sun-bleached
beauty of the Greek ships: how
could I have power if
I had no wish
to transform you: as
you loved my body,
as you found there
passion we held above
all other gifts, in that single moment
over honor and hope, over
loyalty, in the name of that bond
I refuse you
such feeling for your wife
as will let you
rest with her, I refuse you
sleep again
if I cannot have you.

CIRCE'S GRIEF

In the end, I made myself
known to your wife as
a god would, in her own house, in
Ithaca, a voice
without a body: she
paused in her weaving, her head turning
first to the right, then left
though it was hopeless of course
to trace that sound to any
objective source: I doubt
she will return to her loom
with what she knows now. When
you see her again, tell her
this is how a god says goodbye:
if I am in her head forever
I am in your life forever.

PENELOPE'S STUBBORNNESS

A bird comes to the window. It's a mistake
to think of them
as birds, they are so often
messengers. That is why, once they
plummet to the sill, they sit
so perfectly still, to mock
patience, lifting their heads to sing
poor lady, poor lady, their three-note
warning, later flying
like a dark cloud from the sill to the olive grove.
But who would send such a weightless being
to judge my life? My thoughts are deep
and my memory long; why would I envy such freedom
when I have humanity? Those
with the smallest hearts have
the greatest freedom.

TELEMACHUS' CONFESSION

They
were not better off
when he left; ultimately
I was better off. This
amazed me, not because I was convinced
I needed them both but because
long into adulthood I retained
something of the child's
hunger for ritual. How else address
that sense of being
insufficiently loved? Possibly
all children are
insufficiently loved; I
wouldn't know. But all along
they each wanted something
different from me: having
to fabricate the being
each required in any
given moment was
less draining than
having to be
two people. And after awhile
I realized I *was*
actually a person; I had
my own voice, my own perceptions, though
I came to them late. I no longer regret
the terrible moment in the fields,
the ploy that took
my father away. My mother
grieves enough for us all.

VOID

I figured out why you won't buy furniture.
You won't buy furniture because you're depressed.

I'll tell you what's wrong with you: you're not
gregarious. You should
look at yourself; the only time you're totally happy
is when you cut up a chicken.

Why can't we talk about what I want to talk about?
Why do you always change the subject?

You hurt my feelings. I do *not* mistake
reiteration for analysis.

You should take one of those chemicals,
maybe you'd write more.
Maybe you have some kind of void syndrome.

You know why you cook? Because
you like control. A person who cooks is a person who likes
to create debt.

Actual people! Actual human beings
sitting on our chairs in our living room!
I'll tell you what: I'll learn
bridge.

Don't think of them as guests, think of them
as extra chickens. You'd like it.
If we had more furniture
you'd have more control.

TELEMACHUS' BURDEN

Nothing
was exactly difficult because
routines develop, compensations
for perceived
absences and omissions. My mother
was the sort of woman
who let you know she was suffering and then
denied that suffering since in her view
suffering was what slaves did; when
I tried to console her,
to relieve her misery, she
rejected me. I now realize
if she'd been capable of honesty
she would have been
a Stoic. Unfortunately
she was a queen, she wanted it understood
at every moment she had chosen
her own destiny. She would have had to be
insane to choose that destiny. Well,
good luck to my father, in my opinion
a stupid man if he expects
his return to diminish
her isolation; perhaps
he came back for that.

PARABLE OF THE SWANS

On a small lake off
the map of the world, two
swans lived. As swans,
they spent eighty percent of the day studying
themselves in the attentive water and
twenty percent ministering to the beloved
other. Thus
their fame as lovers stems
chiefly from narcissism, which leaves
so little leisure for
more general cruising. But
fate had other plans: after ten years, they hit
slimy water; whatever the filth was, it
clung to the male's plumage, which turned
instantly gray; simultaneously,
the true purpose of his neck's
flexible design revealed itself. So much
action on the flat lake, so much
he's missed! Sooner or later in a long
life together, every couple encounters
some emergency like this, some
drama which results
in harm. This
occurs for a reason: to test
love and to demand
fresh articulation of its complex terms.
So it came to light that the male and female
flew under different banners: whereas
the male believed that love
was what one felt in one's heart
the female believed

love was what one did. But this is not
a little story about the male's
inherent corruption, using as evidence the swan's
sleazy definition of purity. It is
a story of guile and innocence. For ten years
the female studied the male; she dallied
when he slept or when he was
conveniently absorbed in the water,
while the spontaneous male
acted casually, on
the whim of the moment. On the muddy water
they bickered awhile, in the fading light,
until the bickering grew
slowly abstract, becoming
part of their song
after a little longer.

PURPLE BATHING SUIT

I like watching you garden
with your back to me in your purple bathing suit:
your back is my favorite part of you,
the part furthest away from your mouth.

You might give some thought to that mouth.
Also to the way you weed, breaking
the grass off at ground level
when you should pull it up by the roots.

How many times do I have to tell you
how the grass spreads, your little
pile notwithstanding, in a dark mass which
by smoothing over the surface you have finally
fully obscured? Watching you

stare into space in the tidy
rows of the vegetable garden, ostensibly
working hard while actually
doing the worst job possible, I think

you are a small irritating purple thing
and I would like to see you walk off the face of the earth
because you are all that's wrong with my life
and I need you and I claim you.

PARABLE OF FAITH

Now, in twilight, on the palace steps
the king asks forgiveness of his lady.

He is not
duplicitous; he has tried to be
true to the moment; is there another way of being
true to the self?

The lady
hides her face, somewhat
assisted by shadows. She weeps
for her past; when one has a secret life,
one's tears are never explained.

Yet gladly would the king bear
the grief of his lady: his
is the generous heart,
in pain as in joy.

Do you know
what forgiveness means? It means
the world has sinned, the world
must be pardoned—

REUNION

When Odysseus has returned at last
unrecognizable to Ithaca and killed
the suitors swarming the throne room,
very delicately he signals to Telemachus
to depart: as he stood twenty years ago,
he stands now before Penelope.
On the palace floor, wide bands of sunlight turning
from gold to red. He tells her
nothing of those years, choosing to speak instead
exclusively of small things, as would be
the habit of a man and woman long together:
once she sees who he is, she will know what he's done.
And as he speaks, ah,
tenderly he touches her forearm.

THE DREAM

I had the wierdest dream. I dreamed we were married again.

You talked a lot. You kept saying things like *this is realistic.*
When I woke up, I started reading all my old diaries.

I thought you hated diaries.

I keep them when I'm miserable. Anyway,
all those years I thought we were so happy
I had a lot of diaries.

Do you ever think about it? Do you ever wonder
if the whole thing was a mistake? Actually,
half the guests said that at the wedding.

I'll tell you something I never told you:
I took a valium that night.

I keep thinking of how we used to watch television,
how I would put my feet in your lap. The cat would sit
on top of them. Doesn't that still seem
an image of contentment, of well being? So
why couldn't it go on longer?

Because it was a dream.

OTIS

A beautiful morning; nothing
died in the night.
The Lights are putting up their bean tepees.
Rebirth! Renewal! And across the yard,
very quietly, someone is playing Otis Redding.

Now the great themes
come together again: I am twenty-three, riding the subways
in pursuit of Chassler, of my lost love, clutching
my own record, because I have to hear
this exact sound no matter where I land, no matter
whose apartment—whose apartments
did I visit that summer? I have no idea
where I'm going, about to leave New York, to live
in paradise, as I have then
no concept of change, no slightest sense of what would
happen to Chassler, to obsessive need, my one thought being
the only grief that touched mine was Otis' grief.

Look, the tepees
are standing: Steven
has balanced them the first try.
Now the seeds go in, there is Anna
sitting in the dirt with the open packet.

This is the end, isn't it?
And you are here with me again, listening with me: *the sea*
no longer torments me; the self
I wished to be is the self I am.

THE WISH

Remember that time you made the wish?

     I make a lot of wishes.

The time I lied to you
about the butterfly. I always wondered
what you wished for.

     What do you think I wished?

I don't know. That I'd come back,
that we'd somehow be together in the end.

     I wished for what I always wish for.
     I wished for another poem.

PARABLE OF THE GIFT

My friend gave me
a fuschia plant, expecting
much of me, in cold April
judgment not to leave it
overnight in nature, deep
pink in its plastic
basket—I have
killed my gift, exposed
flowers in a mass of leaves,
mistaking it
for part of nature with
its many stems: what
do I do with you now,
former living thing
that last night still
resembled my friend, abundant
leaves like her fluffy hair
although the leaves had
a reddish cast: I see her
climbing the stone steps in spring dusk
holding the quivering
present in her hands, with
Eric and Daphne following
close behind, each
bearing a towel of lettuce leaves:
so much, so much to celebrate
tonight, as though she were saying
here is the world, that should be
enough to make you happy.

HEART'S DESIRE

        I want to do two things:
        I want to order meat from Lobel's
        and I want to have a party.

You hate parties. You hate
any group bigger than four.

        If I hate it
        I'll go upstairs. Also
        I'm only inviting people who can cook.
        Good cooks and all my old lovers.
        Maybe even your ex-girlfriends, except
        the exhibitionists.

If I were you,
I'd start with the meat order.

        We'll have buglights in the garden.
        When you look into people's faces
        you'll see how happy they are.
        Some are dancing, maybe
        Jasmine in her Himalayan anklet.
        When she gets tired, the bells drag.

        It will be spring again; all
        the tulips will be opening.

The point isn't whether or not
the guests are happy.

The point is whether or not
they're dead.

      Trust me: no one's
      going to be hurt again.
      For one night, affection
      will triumph over passion. The passion
      will all be in the music.

      If you can hear the music
      you can imagine the party.
      I have it all planned: first
      violent love, then
      sweetness. First *Norma*
      then maybe the Lights will play.

A NOTE ABOUT THE AUTHOR

Louise Glück teaches at Williams College and lives in Vermont. She is the author of six books of poems and a collection of essays, entitled *Proofs & Theories,* which won the Pen/Martha Albrand Award. She has been the recipient of the National Book Critics Circle Award for Poetry, the Boston Globe Literary Press Award for Poetry, and the Poetry Society of America's Melville Kane Award and William Carlos Williams Award. She is a Fellow of the American Academy of the Arts and Sciences. Her early work has recently been reissued in one volume, *The First Four Books of Poems.* In 1993, she received the Pulitzer Prize for her book *The Wild Iris.*